Time
TRAVEL

Lisa Arias

Educational Media

rourkeeducationalmedia.com

Scan for Related Titles
and Teacher Resources

Before Reading:

Building Academic Vocabulary and Background Knowledge

Before reading a book, it is important to tap into what your child or students already know about the topic. This will help them develop their vocabulary, increase their reading comprehension, and make connections across the curriculum.

1. *Look at the cover of the book. What will this book be about?*
2. *What do you already know about the topic?*
3. *Let's study the Table of Contents. What will you learn about in the book's chapters?*
4. *What would you like to learn about this topic? Do you think you might learn about it from this book? Why or why not?*
5. *Use a reading journal to write about your knowledge of this topic. Record what you already know about the topic and what you hope to learn about the topic.*
6. *Read the book.*
7. *In your reading journal, record what you learned about the topic and your response to the book.*
8. *After reading the book complete the activities below.*

Content Area Vocabulary
Read the list. What do these words mean?

calendar
centuries
decades
elapsed time
end time
interval
leap year
span
start time
timeline
unit

After Reading:

Comprehension and Extension Activity

After reading the book, work on the following questions with your child or students in order to check their level of reading comprehension and content mastery.

1. *How does the mountain, hill, and rock method help you find elapsed time? (Summarize)*
2. *What are the differences between years, decades, and centuries? (Summarize)*
3. *Why do we need to know about elapsed time? (Text to self connection)*
4. *How does skip counting connect with elapsed time? (Asking questions)*
5. *Explain how you find elapsed time within the same hour. (Summarize)*

Extension Activity

Let's test what you know! Using the mountain, hills, and rocks method for elapsed time, calculate how much time you are in class. What time do you start school? What time do you leave? The beginning goes on one side of the page and the end goes on the other side of the page. When you are calculating elapsed time don't forget about the intervals throughout the day for lunch and recess.

Table of Contents

Time

Sometimes time goes fast, sometimes it goes slow.

But no matter what you do
time has a way of sneaking up on you.

Clocks and Calendars

Time is measured using different units. Clocks are just fine to measure smaller units of time like seconds, minutes, and hours.

60 seconds in a minute

60 minutes in a hour

24 hours in a day

Calendars measure larger units of time like days, weeks, months, years, **decades**, and **centuries**.

7 days in a week

365 days in a year

52 weeks in a year

12 months in a year

10 years in a decade

100 years in a century

Timelines

Using a **timeline** is just the right tool
to calculate **elapsed time** for me and you.

Elapsed time is the amount of time that
passes between one point and another.

Timelines can be used just like clocks,
but they count time using mountains, hills, and rocks!

1
Hour
Mountains

5 or 10
Minutes
Hills

1
Minute
Rocks

Same Hour Elapsed Time

Time to try out a same hour elapsed timeline. This timeline is helpful when all you have to track are minutes within the same hour.

How much time passes between 7:18 and 7:44?

Begin your timeline with the starting and ending times.
Draw minute rocks until you count up to a number that ends in zero.

Draw 10-minute hills until you reach your ending time with only single minutes remaining.

Finish counting up with minute rocks until you reach the ending time.

7:18   1   1   10   10   1   1   1   1   **7:44**
7:19   7:20   7:30   7:40   7:41   7:42   7:43   7:44

To calculate the elapsed time, count by tens and then add the ones.

There are 26 minutes between 7:18 and 7:44.

Saving time is always a treat.
Find the elapsed time by subtracting the minutes nice and neat!

$$44 - 18 = 26$$

Same Minute Elapsed Time

No matter the minute, as long as they agree, a timeline of mountains shows elapsed time quite easily.

How much time passes from 11:45 a.m. until 3:45 p.m.?

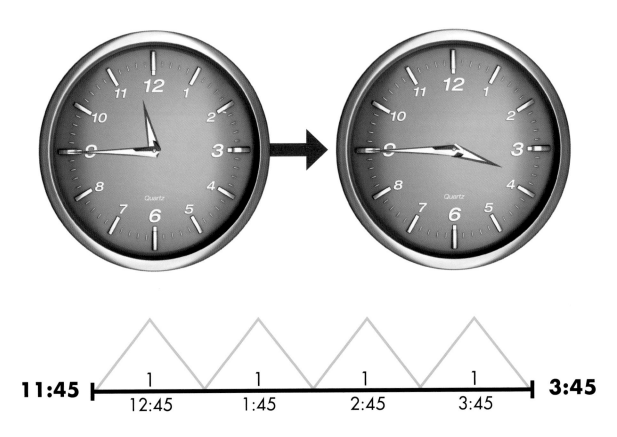

Begin your timeline with the starting and ending times.
Draw an hour mountain for each hour that you count until you reach the ending time.

To calculate the elapsed time, count each mountain. As you can see, four hours pass between 11:45 a.m. and 3:45 p.m.

Time to find school time elapsed time.

School begins at 8:15 a.m. and ends at 2:15 p.m.
How long is the school day?

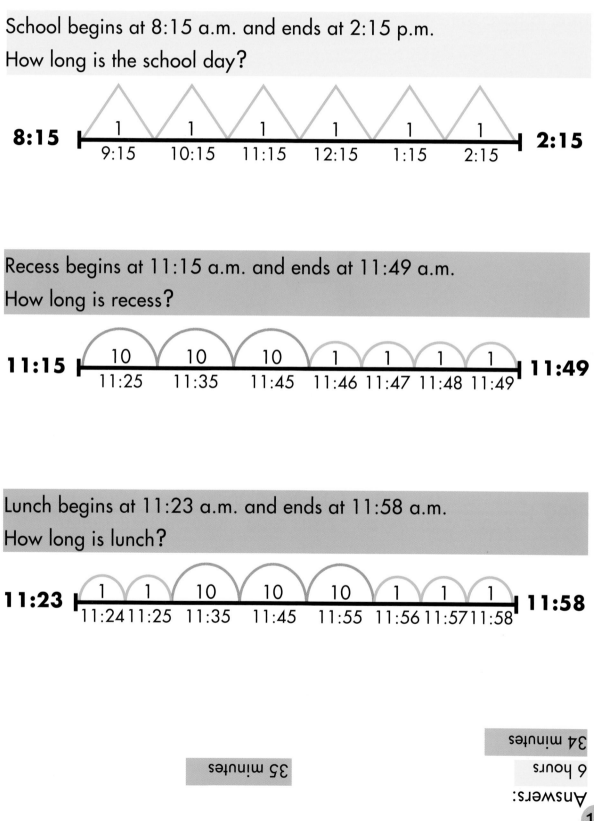

8:15 | 1 | 1 | 1 | 1 | 1 | 1 | **2:15**
9:15 10:15 11:15 12:15 1:15 2:15

Recess begins at 11:15 a.m. and ends at 11:49 a.m.
How long is recess?

11:15 | 10 | 10 | 10 | 1 | 1 | 1 | 1 | **11:49**
11:25 11:35 11:45 11:46 11:47 11:48 11:49

Lunch begins at 11:23 a.m. and ends at 11:58 a.m.
How long is lunch?

11:23 | 1 | 1 | 10 | 10 | 10 | 1 | 1 | 1 | **11:58**
11:24 11:25 11:35 11:45 11:55 11:56 11:57 11:58

Elapsed Time in Hours and Minutes

Time to have some fun counting time with rocks, hills, and mountains.

How much time passes from 4:40 p.m. until 8:37 p.m.?

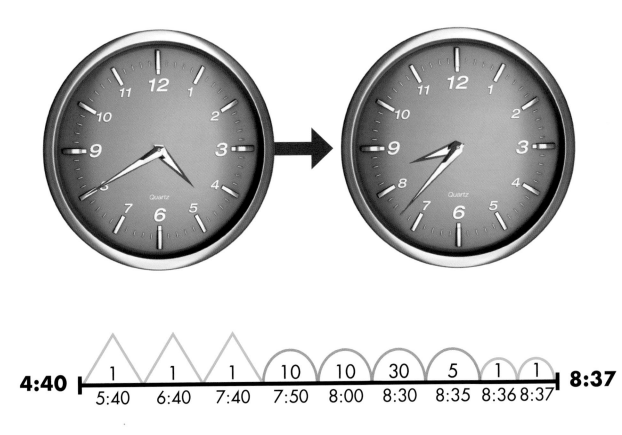

Begin by counting hours until there are only minutes remaining.
Count up until you reach 8:00 (the hour of the ending time).
Count the remaining minutes until the ending time.
To calculate the elapsed time, add the hours and then add the
minutes. As you can see, 3 hours and 57 minutes pass from 5:40 p.m.
until 8:37 p.m.

Time to find elapsed time!

The baseball game began at 6:04 p.m. and ended at 9:26 p.m. How long was the game?

6:04 | 1 (7:04) 1 (8:04) 1 (9:04) 10 (9:14) 10 (9:24) 1 (9:25) 1 (9:26) | 9:26

Swim practice was from 3:11 p.m. until 5:03 p.m. How long was swim practice?

3:11 | 1 (4:11) 10 (4:21) 10 (4:31) 10 (4:41) 10 (4:51) 10 (5:01) 1 (5:02) 1 (5:03) | 5:03

The movie began at 4:58 p.m. and ended at 6:42 p.m. How long was the movie?

4:58 | 1 (5:58) 1 (5:59) 1 (6:00) 30 (6:30) 10 (6:40) 1 (6:41) 1 (6:42) | 6:42

Elapsed Time with Intervals

Intervals are breaks in time and are not included in elapsed time. Let's take a peek at how to calculate elapsed time with intervals.

School begins at 8:15 a.m. and ends at 2:00 p.m. Students leave their classroom from 11:30 a.m. until 1:15 p.m. for lunch, recess, and art. How much time during the day are students in their classroom?

You can create a timeline with a break in it to account for the **interval**.

Begin your timeline with the starting time until the starting time of the interval. Restart the timeline with the ending time of the interval. To calculate, add the hours and minutes. Students are in their classroom for 4 hours each day.

Some intervals will only note the amount of time away. For these intervals, create a timeline with the starting and ending times. Once complete, deduct the time away.

School begins at 8:15 a.m. and ends at 2:00 p.m. Students leave their classroom for a field trip for 3 hours and 25 minutes. How much time did students spend in their classroom?

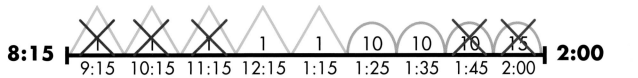

8:15 | 9:15 10:15 11:15 12:15 1:15 1:25 1:35 1:45 2:00 | 2:00

Students spent 2 hours and 20 minutes in their classroom on the day of the field trip.

Find End Times

Now it is time to find out what end times are all about.
Timelines are helpful tools used to find the end times of things we do.

If the movie begins at 5:45 p.m. and lasts for 2 hours and 37 minutes, what time will the movie be over?

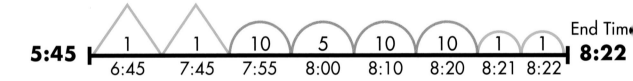

Make your timeline with the **start time**. Add mountains, hills, and rocks for all of the time needed. Count up the time as you go and your timeline will end with the **end time**.

The movie will be over at 8:22 p.m.

Find each end time.

If you leave for school at 7:35 a.m. and it takes 28 minutes to get to school, what time will you arrive at school?

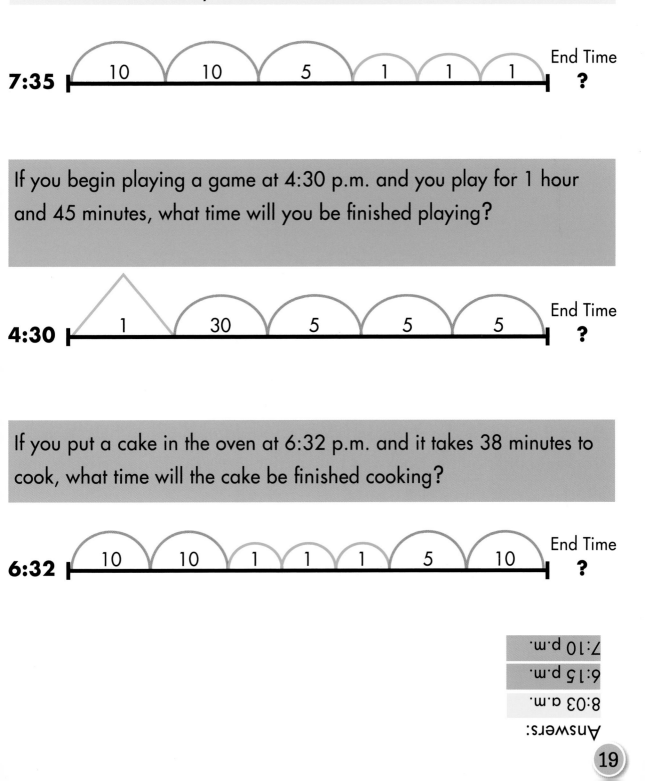

7:35 10 10 5 1 1 1 End Time **?**

If you begin playing a game at 4:30 p.m. and you play for 1 hour and 45 minutes, what time will you be finished playing?

4:30 1 30 5 5 5 End Time **?**

If you put a cake in the oven at 6:32 p.m. and it takes 38 minutes to cook, what time will the cake be finished cooking?

6:32 10 10 1 1 1 5 10 End Time **?**

Find Start Times

Creating a timeline from finish to start is just what to do to find the right start time for me and you!

If you finished playing outside at 6:45 p.m. and played for 1 hour and 35 minutes, what time did you begin playing outside?

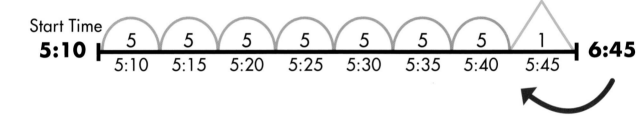

Start the timeline from the end time and add mountains, hills, and rocks, counting time backward in small chunks until you arrive at the start.

Find each start time.

A movie ended at 7:35 p.m. and was 1 hour and 53 minutes long. What time did the movie start?

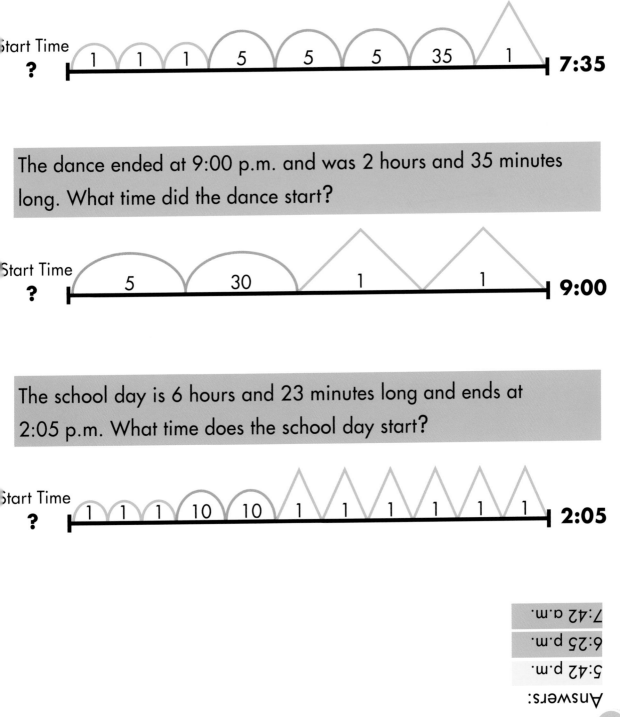

Start Time
? | 1 | 1 | 1 | 5 | 5 | 5 | 35 | 1 | **7:35**

The dance ended at 9:00 p.m. and was 2 hours and 35 minutes long. What time did the dance start?

Start Time
? | 5 | 30 | 1 | 1 | **9:00**

The school day is 6 hours and 23 minutes long and ends at 2:05 p.m. What time does the school day start?

Start Time
? | 1 | 1 | 1 | 10 | 10 | 1 | 1 | 1 | 1 | 1 | 1 | **2:05**

Calendar Time

Calendars are the best tool to use when finding the elapsed time for days, weeks, and months.

Before we begin, let's be smart and look at some charts.

7 days in a week

12 months in a year

365 days in a year

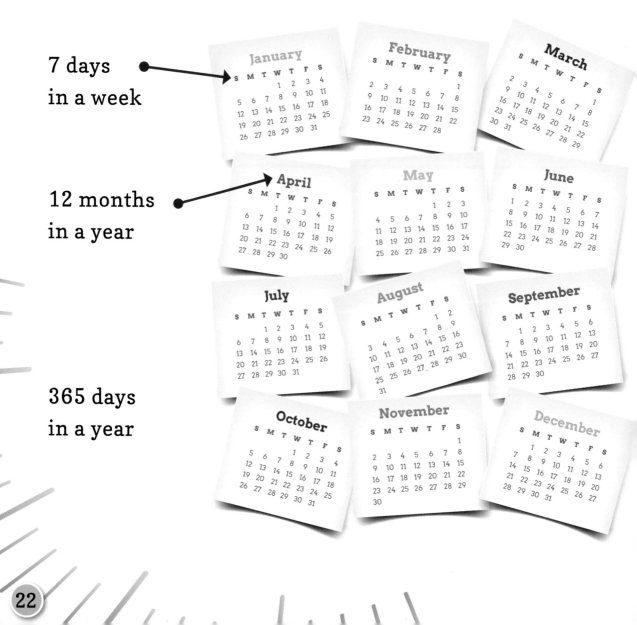

How Many Days in a Month?

Not all months are created equal.

No need to worry because now you will see
how to remember the days in a month quite easily.

January February March April May June July

August September October November December

Months that land
on a finger have
31 days.

Months (except
February) that land
between fingers
have 30 days.

Check It Out!

A **leap year** is a year with 366 days.
It happens every 4 years. February
usually has 28 days, but on a leap year,
it has 29 days.

It is time to find out
what elapsed **calendar** time is all about.

Timelines using mountains, hills,
and rocks are still helpful tools
used to find the elapsed time for me and you.

Winter break began on December 18 and students returned on January 5. How many days were students off from school?

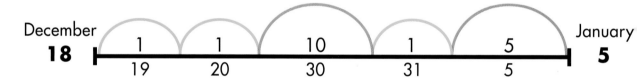

Begin with the start date and count up by days until the last day of December. Next, continue counting up days until January 5. To find the elapsed time, add the days found in the rocks and hills.

Students were away from school for 18 days.

A school year begins September 15 and ends May 15. How many months long is a school year?

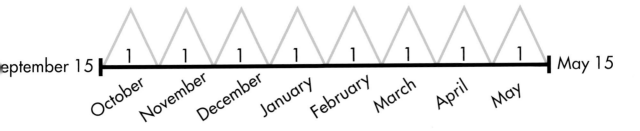

Count up using mountains for each month. The school year is 8 months.

A project was assigned on October 12. Students were given three nights to complete the project for homework. What date is the homework project due?

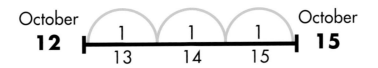

Count up using rocks for each homework night. The project is due on October 15.

Vacation began on July 2 and ended on July 23. How many weeks was the vacation?

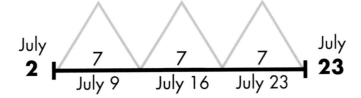

Count up using mountains for each week. The vacation was for 3 weeks.

Years, Decades, and Centuries

Time sure does fly when you are having fun. The fun has arrived and we are ready to count time in years, decades, and centuries.

A decade is a **span** of 10 years.

A century is a span of 100 years. It always runs one **unit** ahead of the actual year because the first century begins with years 0–99.

Years

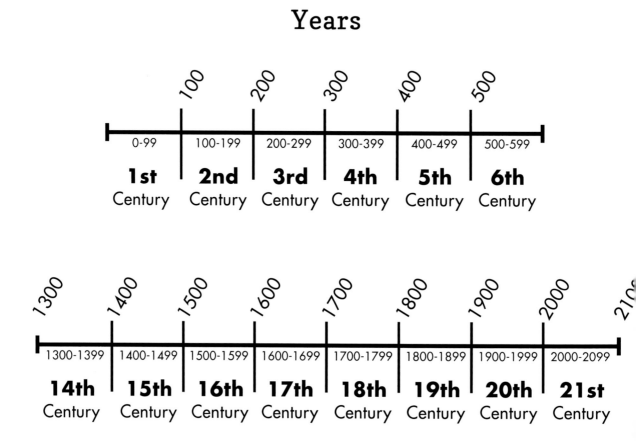

Name the century for each year.

2000

500

451

1492

154

1776

3

1969

Find the elapsed time.

Abraham Lincoln was born on February 12, 1809. How many years old was he on his birthday in 1865?

What century did Abraham Lincoln live in?

Martin Luther King, Jr. was born in 1929 and became the youngest person to receive the Nobel Peace Prize in 1964. How old was he when he received the award?

George Washington was born in 1732 and lived until 1799. How many years did he live?

Answers:

1865 − 1809 = 56
Abraham Lincoln was 56 years old on his birthday in 1865.

Abraham Lincoln lived in the 19th century.

1964 − 1929 = 35
Martin Luther King, Jr. was 35 years old when he received the Nobel Peace Prize.

Glossary

calendar (kal-uhn-dur): table for measuring days, weeks, and years

centuries (SEN-chuh-reez): periods of time equal to 100 years

decades (DEK-ayds): periods of time equal to 10 years

elapsed time (i-lapst TIME): the amount of time that passes between one point and another

end time (END-TIME): the last time of something

interval (IN-tur-vuhl): a break in time between two events

leap year (LEEP-YIHR): a year with 366 days that occurs every four years

start time (START-TIME): the beginning time of something

span (span): a portion of time

timeline (TIME-LINE): a way of listing events in order

unit (YOO-nit): a standard amount used when measuring

Index

Websites to Visit

www.brainpop.com/math/numbersandoperations/elapsedtime/
    preview.weml

www.shodor.org/interactivate/activities/ElapsedTime/

www.sheppardsoftware.com/mathgames/time/mathman_time_elapsed.htm

About the Author

Lisa Arias is a math teacher who lives in Tampa, Florida with her husband and two children. Her out-of-the-box thinking and love for math guided her toward becoming an author. She enjoys playing board games and spending time with family and friends.

Meet The Author!
www.meetREMauthors.com

www.rourkeeducationalmedia.com

PHOTO CREDITS: Cover: © pixelparticle, DNY59, SERGO, proxyminder; Page 4: © brunohaver; Page 5: © Sashkinw, kutberk, Zoran Djekic, pagadesigns; Page 8: © danleap; Page 22: © SERGO; Page 23: © Balavan; Page 29: © Andrew Ostrovsky

Edited by: Jill Sherman

Cover and Interior design by: Tara Raymo

Library of Congress PCN Data

Time Travel: Intervals and Elapsed Time / Lisa Arias
(Got Math!)
ISBN 978-1-62717-706-1 (hard cover)
ISBN 978-1-62717-828-0 (soft cover)
ISBN 978-1-62717-941-6 (e-Book)
Library of Congress Control Number: 2014935583

Printed in the United States of America, North Mankato, Minnesota

Also Available as: